Coins

Andrea Rains
Photographs by Ken O'Donoghue

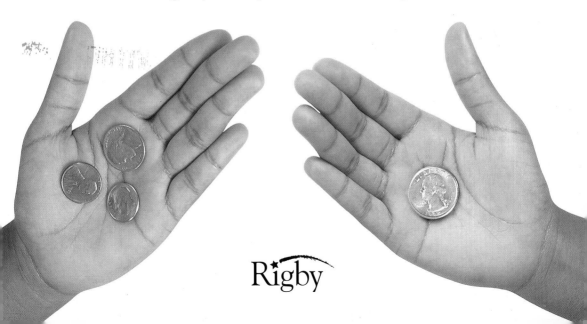

Rigby

Here is a penny.

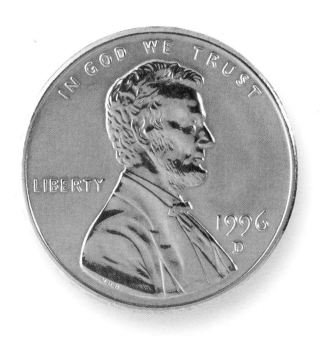

Here is a nickel.

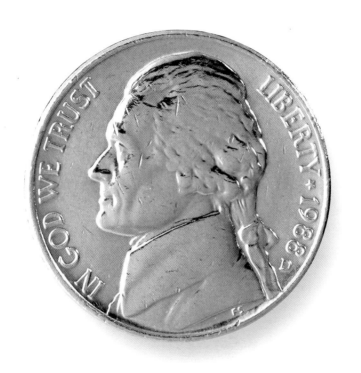

Here is a dime.

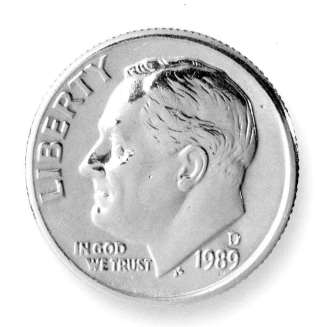

Here is a quarter.

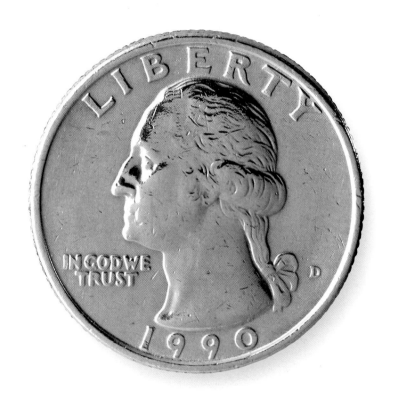

Here is a penny.

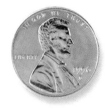

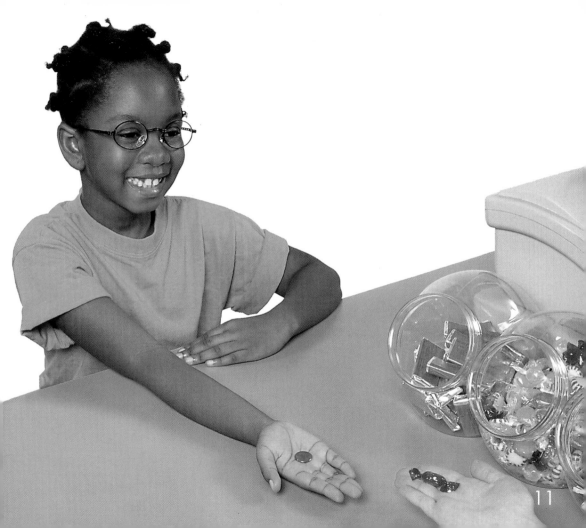

Here is a nickel.

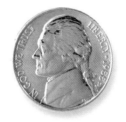

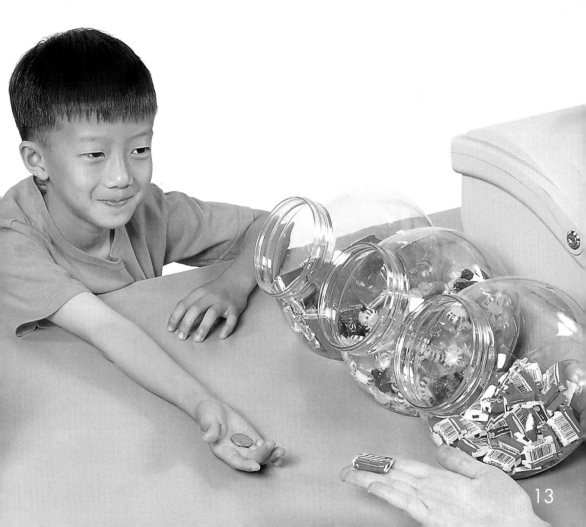

Here is a dime.

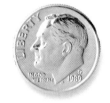

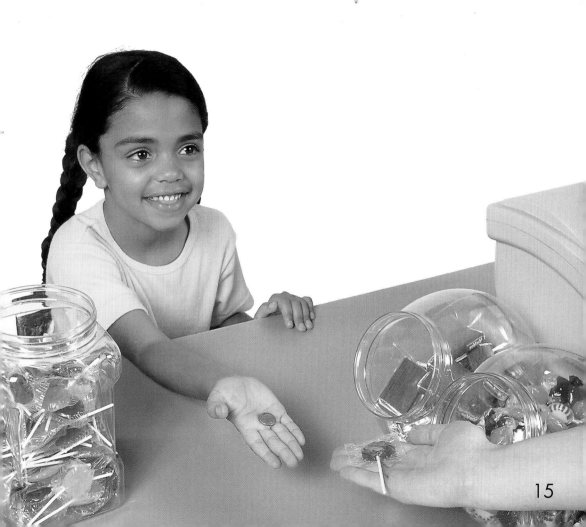

Here is a quarter.

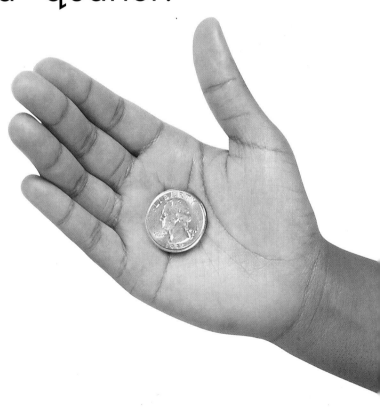